Channeled Messages from Spirit

Christine Diver

Contents

Dedication

This book is dedicated to each and every living soul in this lifetime who is prepared to stand up for what they believe in, to help Mother Earth recover from the damage which has been done and wants to try and make this world a better place.

To every person who has always been told you are lazy, you are useless, this book will hopefully give you some hope that there is a spirit team there stood by you every minute of every day, just waiting to help you, support you, and help you to achieve your life's purpose whatever that may be. All you have to do is ask!

Acknowledgments

There are so many people that need to be mentioned here. First of all, to my guides for sharing this information with us for all to read. Without their knowledge and the wisdom of the ancestors this book would not been able to be made

To all the staff at Amazon Publishing Ltd, for making this project come to life. I thank each and every one of you and I hope you will all achieve anything you set your mind to.

Everyone at Basecamp (HP 2), the whole team there who have helped bring this project to life. The admin/secretarial teams, the illustrators who came up with fantastic front and back covers for me. All the proof reading and editorial teams which made the book the best it could be.

I can't thank you all enough for helping my dream come true.

Hopefully this will give other people hope that even when all the stops are against you, you can still get through any challenge that is presented to you and you can succeed. I hope this book gives people hope and faith that there are people out there who care deeply about Mother Earth and how she is treated.

People who care and people who will be there to listen whenever they are needed.

About the Author

Hi my name is Christine Diver. I am a massive animal lover. I am a reiki practitioner and have been since 2015 and love being a channel for healing, to enable healing to be given to whoever or whatever needs that healing at the time.

I try my best to help the people and the animals that the universe brings to me. And try hard to make the world a better place anyway I can and am honored to be able to work for spirit in this way.

I am very passionate about us all pulling together to help Mother Earth recover from the damage which has been caused. Not just to the land itself but all the beautiful oceans as well.

I accept my part in this path, and always let spirit guide me. We are all divinely guided, and we all have healing gifts, it's just a case of if you choose to follow that path or not.

I hope you love the book as much as I do, and I hope it may bring hope, love and peace, so we can all live in harmony with one another one day.

Messages from the tribes: Migration

The Native Americans were believed to be the first type of people that appeared on this earth after the cave men. They believe everything on this planet has its own spirit from every flower, plant, piece of metal to the moon and the stars in the sky.

The Native Americans were believed to of arrived 15000 years ago in three great migrations. They were said to have arrived via a "land bridge" from Siberia and may have set up home in a region between Siberia and Alaska. This area was said to contain woody plants that could be used to make fires according to a recent study.

Most Native Americans were known to be descended from a small number of migrants that crossed a land bridge between Asia and America during the ice age and grew to populate North and South America. There are now more than 100 different tribes throughout America.

Taken on the 20-11-2016 Part 1

"We came here for the hope of a new life, to have to find a new food source. Our main source of food was fruit, birds and deer. When we first came here, we hunted the mammoth and used their hides for homes, food for our family, and to keep us warm. We hunted with bows and arrows with heads of flint made from stone. We used the fur of the mammoth to keep us warm and for trading purposes to bargain for lands we lived off. The water we fished and washed and cleaned ourselves in the water and used the water to cleanse our souls.

We had no need for arguing and fighting with anyone or anything, we honored mother earth, and father sky, the trees, the plants, and all living things. We only used what we needed to survive. As time went on more people came and we evolved into the tribes that we are today. There was much conflict between our tribes as land and food became scarce.

The white man and soldiers came and took our food and land, killed and hurt our people for their own greed. We were forced to move out of our lands and told to move to where they sent us. Our people were kind, solitary people, but the white man made us angry. We were forced to leave our lands which created much disharmony within our lands. It took us a long time to forgive the white man for what they had done but we did, and we fought for them against rival tribes as we were promised to be able to live in peace on our lands if we did. The white man went against the treaties that were formed and yet again forced us from our lands without choice or respect. We were treated like vermin within their world and treated very badly. All we wanted was to live in peace and harmony as we have always done. We were not happy, and we were forced to live in lands we did not know or choose to live in, but we had no choice.

We are no longer angry with the white man as anger and hate is no longer any good for the soul, we healed ourselves and tried to heal the lands which they had gave us through love, nurture and prayer, we prayed that we would be reunited with our lands once again one day and we know we will. For when our land is nearly destroyed there will be a new tribe of people come to our lands with the force needed to bring our lands back to us and we will be free once again one day. We will be saved, and our land will be saved, before it is destroyed, as mother earth is angry with how she has been treated, and she will be sending new help and support for our people and our lands, and we will be reunited once again.

Teach people to respect the land and the beautiful planet we have been given to live in and rekindle your own love with mother earth and the gifts she has to offer do not heed the white man way of greed and destruction. Be part of a loving peaceful lifestyle, you have no need for material things all you need, and need to nurture yourself and your land is sent from within. Look deep inside yourself and find what you are seeking. Unity and love can all be found within yourself. All you need to do is seek and you will find.

Respect the earth and everything that is within it, and you will be free from the white man and his destruction as you will find everything you need from within. Use your intuition, listen to what you are being told from within. You will be able to acquire everything that you need to survive this depressive situation that is this life now that we live in. We will be here supporting you and guiding you to your right purpose and your right rewards. You need to trust in the information you are given and trust that it is right and direct from the source. You will find what you are all seeking at one stage or another and you will learn how to achieve your inner peace. We thank you for this opportunity for us to teach you and pass on the information that you, and us seek, we will be here to guide you and show you the way. We will teach you our teachings for you to pass on and we will help you on your journey just trust in what you are receiving and know that it is true and just knowledge and that you have the right to pass this knowledge on. You are of Navaho descent, and you will achieve all you are here to achieve.

You, we are here to help with your life purpose, we will be here to guide you, we are here to give the support that you need, and we will help you to move forward and gain the knowledge that you seek.

We are the elders of the Navaho, we are here to teach and guide you, and we are here to help you on your way. Help us to help you. Help us to keep our lifetimes alive and keep our children knowledgeable about their journeys and life purpose.

We are the Waccamaw tribe from North Carolina and we are here to help you along your way. Help us to understand your language and we will help you understand ours. And we can and will work together to get our promised lands back to where they belong and we will receive our lands back before it gets disturbed beyond recognition, we are on our way but need people like yourself to enable us to do that. Your rewards are on their way, you will receive what you ask for as you are staying true to your purpose and will be rewarded greatly. We are helping and assisting with that, as we speak, they are on their way. We thank you again for this opportunity to help us with our purpose and would like to thank every one of you for listening to us and we would like to say goodbye now until our next discussion. Thank you"

Running bear, Black eagle, Navajo elders, and Sioux tribe elders.

Taken in the 20-11-2016 Part 2

"We are the Navajo tribe we have come also to help you on your journey, we have come to give you the information that you seek, we came here after the first set of people, we came because of the land and opportunity for the life we wished to live, we came to serve the land and help our families and friends recover, we needed to find new lands and herbs to help and develop our lives we came to try and help mother earth recover from the ice age to help the land to recover and to help the land start anew, as we are all part of the same circle of life, we all need to do our part in keeping the land and earth we need to survive healthy and true we need to keep our lands free from poison so our fish can survive and renew so we can survive we need to help save mother earth as she is beginning to die and action needs to be taken to help and assist in these matters as mother earth is angry and finding it hard to recover from the damage man has caused on her own we need to help and assist her in doing this.

Without her we have no plants, with no plants we will not have oxygen and will not be able to breathe. We need to revive and renew her lands and help her to start over again for if we don't have mother earth we do not survive. We have no way of surviving without air in our lungs without air to breathe we will all die, and our race will become extinct as man is making the animals to become extinct, we will all soon perish if something is not done. We will all suffer the consequences of man's actions. We need to help get our knowledge out there to help revive our nation before we all disappear. We need to all come together and unite against the catastrophe that is becoming. We need to unite for our race to unite and survive. We need to breathe the air back into our lands and seas to help it to regain its strength and fight against the poison that is pollution and poisoning of the land's animals and all living things. Time is beginning to run out, more and more destruction and disruption will come if something is not done.

We need to unite and stop fighting, competing, and arguing with each other as none of this is going to serve the cause which is to help mother earth regain her strength that is slowly swindling away. We need to help her recover from the destruction that has already been incurred and try and prevent what is to come. We need to unite as one with the universe, awaken each other's souls of passion which will uncover what part every one of us must play in the renewing of this plain, and the next, we will have no planet earth to learn our valuable lessons on if we don't do something soon.

We need to come up with a plan for us to enable us to do this as there will be no time left if we do not act soon, we are here to help you with that plan to help teach and show people a new way for them to survive. We are here to teach them how to survive the old way where there is no need for such vanity, greed, and destruction we have been placed in this world to bring unity back to this land and the people, to help dissolve the anger, hate, rage, and upset and change it for joy, peace, laughter, and calm. We are here to teach you how to find your inner calm, and find your inner strength, to remind you of who and how we are meant to be, how we are meant to be living as we have all seem to of forgotten our true purpose and who we are and most of all, what we are here to do, we are here to help you learn and survive this trivial world that is now a world of destruction and hate and revive it back to one of love as it should be,

We are here to help you do that and teach you our ways to help you and assist you, we are here to help you with the new wave of children who are already starting to make an appearance.

The rainbow warriors are on their way and will be starting to evolve now shortly and we are here to help you identify those children and teach how to help them with their purpose and help you to understand their characters and abilities and learn you why they are here and how to best help them to achieve their purpose and help them along their way. We will teach you how to work with these children and how to teach others how to deal and handle them on yours, and their paths we will help you to understand these special force which are on their way to pave way for the world to be put right once again to unite the rest of the world in a new understanding as to how to acquire yourself with the tools you need to help you with your purpose and goals."

The time In between

During the last seven years a lot has gone on. I have had to do a lot of personal healing, due to the death of my father, horse and brother.

Apologies for not being in touch I have spent the last seven years getting myself back on track. But there have also been some positive things that happen in my time away. I have been doing voluntary work for Hope charity as an admin volunteer, I have been a volunteer for Coventry Mind, and have been a befriender, befriending elderly people and have really enjoyed this. I was debating being a Care worker as I enjoyed the befriender work. but have since decided my services would be best used being a Chanell for Spirit, and completing the book we started way back in 2016.

So, apologies for being away so long. But I am now ready to continue the teachings that you wish to tell us. I am very curious to see what you must teach us all, and I am ready and willing to be the Channell you need for you to get your information out there. So, I invite my spirit guides and the elders to now come and work with me as a Channel for you.

Rainbow children

17-07-2024

"Good evening Christine and thank you so much for coming back to us and giving us this opportunity to speak. As we have watched you have been through many battles which you have got through, we are so proud of what you have gone through personally and are glad you decided to come back to write our teachings for us."

"When we last spoke, we told you about the rainbow warriors, these are a special type of child and adult that are incarnating into this world at this time to create change. They are very high-spirited individuals and do not confide in the laws of the country, as they are here to create change. Our poor mother earth has suffered dearly, we are polluting her waters, we are killing her animals to extinction, and it must stop. The rainbow warriors are a band of warriors who will be coming to create change and they will be individuals who will in time get into places of power, through teaching, and creating new laws and rules which will work towards a brighter and more peaceful resolution to the many troubles that mother earth has had many challenges to deal with. She is angry at the people of this land who have caused so much destruction to her beautiful planet.

The rainbow warriors have been sent to incarnate in this lifetime at this time so they can help awaken others, to the corruption that is our government, and our rule books have led them to believe. They are a new type of people who have incarnated currently to help mother earth to recover from the destruction she has received and are here to teach people the old ways. They are here to restore the balance between the man and the planet. They are here to help awaken people to a new way, a more peaceful way, but before this there is much change that needs to be created. This will take time to achieve as there is a very big mess that the rainbow warrior must clean up. The planet is in danger of dying and so are we if nothing is done. What will happen when they have poisoned the last of our waters so their crops cannot grow, what will they do when there is no food, when all the supermarkets close as they have no stock to fill them? What will they do when they have cut the last tree down, so we have no oxygen to breathe? This is why the rainbow warriors are here. They are here to awaken people and help them to remember what they always knew, how to live off the land. To awaken people to the world of spirit, to awaken people to the possibility of a new and possible way of life if we all work together. The rainbow warriors are peace makers as well as warriors. The warriors are here to create the change that needs to happen, and the peacemakers are here to teach the people how to live-in tune with the land once more and remind them of the knowledge they already know, that their ancestors have taught them. They are here to awaken people to spirit and teach people how to be in tune with the land to restore balance. As the whole world has gone out of balance because people have forgotten that we are all part of the same cycle of life, and make people realize that what they do to the mother earth they also do to themselves, they need to realize how to commune with the other energies on the planet. The stone people, the plant kingdom and the animal kingdom. They all have great knowledge and wisdom which we can call upon at any time to help us. There is not a condition in this world that there isn't a cure too if you teach the medicine of the plant kingdom and address the spiritual causes of the disease and sickness. We are here to help you to do this. We will teach you our ways, and we will teach you again how to be at one with the land so that the world can return to a state of balance, and we thank you for allowing us this opportunity to be able to do this. We appreciate that you wish to help and wish to be a channel for us so that we can pass this valuable knowledge to you so you can pass it onto others. It has come to a stage now where we are having to find new ways to pass this knowledge on, and you are from Navajo lineage, you have lived as a Navajo in previous lifetimes and do not worry, you do have the permission of the elders to pass this information on. I know you were worried about being able to share the information as you are not an elder, but it has come to light that in order for us to bring the world back into balance we need people like yourself that are prepared to write our words for us as we are in the spirit world and have no physical bodies anymore. We have all lived on Earth at one point or another and have learnt many things over the years of watching the world as it is now, and it saddens us greatly that we are even having to have this conversation and that mother earth is so badly damaged. There is progress being made but it is unfortunately slow and will no doubt take many more lifetimes to get the world back into balance."

"A shaman's path is a difficult path, and we are so glad that you have decided to be part of this process. We are so glad that you have passed every one of the challenges and initiations that you have had. Michael indeed did test you to your limits but you got through it, he should never of done what he did and we won't go into detail here, but we are so proud of you that you overcome this difficulty and returned to your loving compassionate self even after everything that has happened, you have indeed stuck to your rightful pass and have stayed true to your heart and your soul. Your twin flame has been brought back into your life as a reward for all your hard work, and all the challenges you have overcome. He is to treat you right and to restore your faith in love. It will not be an easy path for both of you, but together we know you will succeed in every challenge you are set, and you will shine your combined light as a path for people who have been in the dark. They will see your light as a path to lead them back to their own rightful paths. You indeed have been brought back together to help heal each other, which will only make your bond and love even stronger. There is no love stronger than the love of a twin flame, Michael was indeed your false twin. He taught you the most important lessons of your life so far of your journey. There are still many lessons and challenges to face but together you will face them to the best of your ability as you always do. You will be greatly rewarded for all your hard work. We thank you for being brave enough to walk a shaman's path, to help restore the balance to this world, and to heal yourself and your ancestral karma also. It has and will not be an easy journey, but you are more than capable of dealing with any challenge we present you with. You were chosen to do this job because of your strong warrior personality, and through that warrior personality it will help you to identify with the other rainbow warriors of your time. You are all unique in your abilities and strengths, and you will learn how to develop and grow those strengths and will be shown your weaknesses so that you may overcome them to be the best version of yourself that you can be, for your highest good and the highest good of all."

"We are going to leave it there for tonight now as we wish not to overload you with too much information in one sitting. We will speak again soon."

"God bless, Sioux and Navajo elders."

Creation

19-07-2024

"Good morning, Christine and thank you for taking the time to listen to what we have to say. Today we would like to talk about the creation of the world. Now these tales vary from tribe to tribe but some of the things that are combined in all tribes are the fact that the world was created through the union of Mother Earth and Father Sky. Mother Earth would create different worlds, and Father Sky would create the life force that is within us all, and the great spirit /divine creator would create the soul/spirit that lives within all of us, so that each person had a piece of the great spirit within each and every one of us all. The combination of this union created the water which developed into the condensation which then created the clouds which developed the rains which fell into what has become our oceans, and onto mother earth and new life forms began to grow.

The plant kingdom was developed with all the medicinal properties, and through the plant kingdom, The stone kingdom, The mineral kingdom, and the tree people that grew, produced the oxygen that we now breathe.

The Mother created all. The Animal kingdom, the two legged, four legged, and the feathered ones.

The goddess of the ocean took it upon herself to give all the creatures that swam within her oceans everything that they needed to create and build and grow and evolve into the many creatures we have in the oceans to this day.

The Mother Earth then decided that the earth should be shared by humans, she then created the male and female of the land and father sky filled them with his life force, and the Great spirit created their souls, and they became alive.

The male and females then joined in union and reproduced to fill the world as we know it now.

At first, all went well. Our people and the animal kingdom expanded, and we all lived together peacefully. We shared duties. We were taught through the animal kingdom and the plant kingdom how to survive. They agreed to sacrifice themselves for us to survive. The plant people agreed to teach us their medicines providing the land, and they were treated with respect, and not used recklessly. They agreed to provide us with the oxygen we needed to survive. Whenever we would go out to hunt prayers were offered to the animal whether it be Mammoth, Buffalo or deer before the hunt and thanks were given to the animal for their sacrifice.

Father sky and the thunder beings gave us the fire that we needed with their lightning to keep ourselves warm, we were taught by our ancestors how to create fire so that we would have warmth and means to cook the meat which we ate. We were taught by the animal and plant kingdom how to treat the animals with respect, that had sacrificed themselves for us. Our ancestors were taught how to use every part of the animal so that the animal did not lose its life in vain.

The animals' teeth and bones were used to make tools, combined with the Mineral kingdom gave us flint and wood to use to make our arrows and spears so we were able to hunt. The horses agreed for us to be carried on their backs in exchange for food and shelter, and that they were treated with respect. The hides of the animals were stripped, scraped, and dried out to create clothes and warmth. The meat that was edible was eaten and the parts which were not edible were placed bk into mother earth as a gift or were used for medicine purposes. We all lived off the lands and showed great respect to the mother earth and father sky for the great gifts they have gave to us.

Then the settlers came from other parts of the world and came with their machinery ripping up mother earth to create more crops. They tore through mother earth planting their seeds for their crops with no respect for the earth mother, or any of the beautiful gifts that she had given them.

We were forced off our lands by the white man because they wanted our lands for oil, gold, and horticulture purposes, and we were forced to leave our lands. We were forbidden to continue to live life as we had always known it. We were forced to go to White man's schools and not even allowed to speak in our natural language. All our traditions and ceremonies were banned, we were no longer allowed to perform our rituals of thanks and gratitude.

We were angry with what the white man for a very long time. They brought with them diseases that killed off a lot of our people as we did not have the immune system to be able to recover from such diseases as smallpox. A lot of our people were killed by the white man as we tried to defend the lands that we were living on. But we were forced out, and forced to live in a land that was completely alien to us. Our whole way of living had to change. It saddened our hearts, and still does as we see what further destruction man has caused to our mother earth.

There were many wars that broke out between our people and the white man while trying to defend our mother earth and the lives we had been accustomed to living. As the white man took more and more land there was less and less food for our people and wars broke out between the different tribes as food got more and more scarce. Many of our people died through malnutrition as there was not enough food for us to survive. Luckily some fled up the mountains and hid. Those people were the ones that still live off the land today, but the majority of our people were moved out and forced to live on reservations where the white man told us to live. We cried for our mother earth and what they were doing to her. Mother earth was very angry with what they had done to her lands and the gift she had given us. We were angry at the white man for a very long time. We no longer have that anger and belief and know that one day we will get our land back. There will be people sent by mother earth and the star nations which will help us stand together and get our lands back and return the lands back to how it was, and the peoples will start to live back in harmony with the lands and all the spiritual beings that live upon her.

The native people believe that everything on the land has its own life force from the tiniest of stone to the biggest of aircraft, everything has its own life force that has been given by father sky and each and everything has a soul given by the great spirit that should be treated with respect. Unfortunately, that respect has disappeared over the years. We desperately need to remind people that what we do to mother earth we do to ourselves people have forgotten that we are all part of the great circle of life. From mother earth we came and to mother earth we will return.

We thank you for allowing us the opportunity to share our truth with you and the other people upon the mother earth, and we thank you for that, until the next time, God Bless "

Trusting Your Intuition

"Good evening Christine and welcome back to our table we are glad that you have been resting up and had a good holiday today we would like to talk to you about the story of how crow got her feathers. Many years ago crow was a happy go lucky bird he was full of a multiple of colors in his feathers, but one day he decided that he would be clever and try to be like the eagle and fly to the sun. Eagle warned him against this as he may fly too close to the father sun and end up burning his feathers. But she thought she could soar high enough like eagle above the clouds and father sun and continued. Crow flew higher and higher until he got too close to father sun and as she got nearer the sun, her feathers began to darken, her feathers began to get burned. They began to become black like charcoal. Crow she started to panic and she flew back down towards the earth, she was so upset that her beautiful feathers had turned black. Eagle said to her we tried to warn you but you chose not to listen, you should always listen to what the great spirit tells you, your intuition is your guide it is your internal navigator. Crow learnt an important lesson that day as she learnt not only was there is a consequence for e   ach action but also learnt that listening to others is a very important part of being a good leader. Crow was that adamant that she could fly over the sun like eagle that she didn't listen and due to the consequences she was left with black feathers as a reminder that she needs to listen not just to her intuition but to listen to others.

Each and every one of us has the great spirit to guide us. You always have spiritual guidance available to you. We are here to guide you and teach you, we are here to help you to evolve and be the best version of yourself that you can be. The great spirit is within all of us, and we are always divinely guided. Listening to our inner guidance is very important, not only can it save our lives, but it is also our way of communicating with the great spirit. Crow realized that she had made the wrong decision because she had gone against her own intuition and the guidance of others. In order to be an active part of the community we need to be able to communicate and listen to others. We all together will make the right decisions if we listen as we are always divinely guided. Use your intuition to guide you always, if something doesn't feel right don't do it. If someone doesn't feel right, don't trust them as that is your internal navigation trying to show you the right way. It is very important that we always listen to our inner guidance. We as tribal members have all been on the earth and have all had earthly lead lives, we have experienced many things and have much knowledge to share with you. In our tribes telling stories and listening to those stories is how we learn and evolve but the youngsters they are too consumed with technology to want to listen to those stories that's why we are grateful for people like Christine who can channel our messages for us so that the people of today can grow and learn the way we did.

We are very glad that we have been given this opportunity to be able to share our stories with you. We would like to thank Christine for being a channel for our messages and are very grateful to have been given this opportunity.

May the Great Spirit be with all of you, we offer you our unconditional love and hope that we will have many more opportunities to tell our stories."

God Bless xx

Personal Questions and Answer I Had For My Guides

General guidance

05-09-13

"Good evening Christine, I am Crow man of the Sioux tribe. I have come to speak with you to try and restore some of your faith that you have lost at this time. We are here to guide you. We have seen you struggling and have come to assist. You have many worries and doubts at this time, and you are right to pass those worries onto the angels to help and assist you. We are all here to help you on your way, you have much confusion in your mind at this time and we are here to reassure you, everything is in its rightful place at this time, there are many challenges you have gone through and still to go through in the future but please believe as when we say they are all for your greatest good, they are sent to you for you to learn from them so you can evolve to a greatest and highest version of yourself. Matters of the heart and cut deep are always the hardest lessons of them all, but as long as you stay true to heart you will only be sent the same like for like. If you love and respect yourself, you will vibrate to people who love and respect you. You are beginning to doubt in yourself, people will be starting to doubt in you. You have faced many difficult decisions of the heart but trust me you are making all the right choices, and you will reap the rewards of those decisions soon we are sending someone who will help make your dreams happen the people you need and have agreed to help you on your quest animals and humans alike will be with you soon. Just trust keep your faith we know that is difficult for you at this time but just trust you will be provided for; you have stayed solid in you cause and purpose as we knew you would. You need to start to believe in yourself again, you have always stayed pure to heart even when the whole world seemed to be against you. You kept your courage and your strength, you listened to your body, and rested when you needed to this is very important and as far as doubting yourself as a channel well this document tonight should have proved you are indeed a channel and a very good one at that and we appreciate you trusting us to keep you safe and guide you. The unicorns and the fairies are indeed following your cause and are very pleased with your progress it gladdens their hearts to see you being so loving and caring to the beautiful animals and people of this planet and wish to thank you from the bottom of their hearts. Your horse Henry is indeed very pleased and grateful that you have chosen to walk this path along with him so you can both learn and grow, you are indeed a healing team and a mighty team You do make, and he wanted you to know that he loves you very much.

Question for my guides

10-10-17

Is Tarran my true twin flame?

What is the best course of action for me to take regarding the best place for me to move my horse too? As I have been presented with several possibilities and really don't know what opportunities to take as they all have lots of positive change that could assist me, as I'm really confused as to what would be for the best and would really like your assistance and guidance in these matters,

So, if you could please come and assist me now if you would, I call you into my space now to assist me with these matters.

"Good evening, Christine and thank you for coming back to our table. We can see that you are struggling at this time and have come to come and help you and assist you at this time.

You have many questions which you are trying to find answers to. We know you are struggling to receive your guidance currently and have come to assist.

The first question that you seek about your true twin flame, we can tell you at this time you are indeed right about what you think, Taran is indeed your true twin flame you have been placed back in touch as you have much work to do, you will indeed be meeting again soon. We have indeed been helping him with his own journey and he will be back with you again soon and all will become clear, you have both Indeed learnt many lessons throughout your lifetime and we can reassure you that he is ok, he is in his own time of self-reflection, and you will be reunited again soon. We have been assisting him in his journey and he has lived a very troubled time away from you but he is now starting to remember and he will be with you again soon, do not worry, about your previous partner as we are also working with him as well at this time and indeed sending him the support and guidance that he needs at this time, I know you have been worried as to how you and Taran will be able to work together as you know Luke will respond badly but be assured we are always working for you greatest and highest good at all times. Trust in yourself, do not doubt what you feel you are here to do, you will always find your way, you are indeed divinely guided. Try not to worry and just trust that we are always with you, and what you are trying to achieve will always be supported and guided if you stay true to yourself and your purpose. I know you care about Taran very deeply and are fearful for him but do not be afraid, you just keep doing what you are doing, send him the healing that is needed and he will indeed regain his strength, the love you have for him and always have goes much deeper than just this lifetime you have been together through and we can see that the dream of you being a princess confused you as that was with Luke, but Luke is indeed a Karmic relationship that was sent to help you to evolve and to believe in yourself, he gave you many lessons and taught you how to love again and to learn forgiveness and compassion. They are indeed very important lessons and you have indeed evolved well; we are sorry the trauma and heartache you received was caused but as you can see now it was all relevant to bring you and evolve you to where you are now. Your friend Lucy was right, back when you were children you and Taran were not ready or prepared for the tasks that lay ahead of you, you have both evolved now to a more better vibration, I know you have no clue to as to why you received the calling to heal him but you were indeed chosen to do that as we know your love was deep and we knew you would not do nothing he indeed called for you he began to remember the love you shared and began to start his journey back to where he should indeed be, he is still a fair bit away from where he needs to be but be assured he will soon remember what it is he needs to do, he will be guided back to you and you can start your journey together you have a lot of guidance and support to help you all, all will soon become clear as to what and why things have occurred the way they have. I know you are still confused as to what it is you are meant to be doing, and how you and Taran fall together as to the plans which have been laid for you and chosen by yourselves, but all will become clear soon.

As to your horse and what you should do with him. I feel your confusion in this decision about if it is indeed logical for you to move him closer to home as the distance you are travelling indeed affecting yourself. But Sarah can also help you greatly in many ways she can help guide you and help you with your animal communication but there is much work still to be done before this, at this time you need to focus on one thing at time, you are overloading yourself with too many plans and ideas, they are all indeed divinely guided but you are right in what you think the distance you are travelling is taking its toll on you. Sarah is also quite a considerable distance away, but she can guide you, in many decisions that you can and will make.

But for now, you need to focus on being able to get better you will know in your heart what the right decision is, try to open to listen when you go to see your friend Kate you will be helped in your decision trust your intuition as there is much positive work that you could do at kates yard also. Trust your intuition and let it guide you to trust in who you are, what you are here to do.

Wild horse will help you, he is a very wise and respected elder will be there in your heart to help guide you, help yourself by asking him to come and be with you, at the time, ask him what he feels, and ask him to relay that to you, to help you make those decisions. Trust in who you are and what you are here to do.

You know you are here to; help make this world a better place you know and have been told you have a gift for working with the animals, use them and their medicine to help make the world a better place for them, we need the animals they are valuable allies. Learn how to communicate with them so they can help you and guide you, also along your path let them in, let them guide you, you have an open heart that is all you need, ask them to help you call them to help you the same way you call us to give you guidance. Trust in the spiritual team you have around, all you need to do is believe in yourself and what you know to be true in your heart and the hearts of others and the animals trust in what you see, sense, and feel. When you are with the animals ask them to communicate with you and ask them for guidance that they have for you ask them to show you the way the same way you ask us, when you go to them, take your paper and your pens and ask them to assist you and communicate with you, tell them you want to hear their voice and what knowledge they have for you, open yourself up to be able to see and hear the guidance that they have for you and tell them they will be listened to as you would like to be able to give them a voice. The owners may not want to listen but they will still be heard, tell them that you will try and help them the best that you can and tell them you wish to learn the lessons they have to teach you, as with their knowledge you can try to make the world a better place for them, you are here to be able to give mother earth and all her gifts a voice, Learn how to be at one with the lands, learn how to listen to the wind, the rain, the weather learn how to understand what they have to teach you, and the knowledge they have for you. We hope we have helped to answer the questions that you have, and we will be happy to help and guide you whenever you need our assistance, we are always here for you and to help and assist you, and we are grateful for the opportunity to be able to work with you to help us with our cause along with your cause.

We are here to try and help the world to be a better place and to try and save mother earth from the destruction that has been caused we are here to try and put things right and back to how everything should be , there is so many souls that have lost their way and forgotten what it is to respect mother earth and the beautiful gifts she has given us, she is being destroyed and her beautiful animals are being killed and hunted for sports this makes mother earth very sad she gave us these gifts out of love and so we can evolve and to help become who we desired to become, to be reminded that we are all one in the great spirit, we are all part of one creation and people have forgotten that, they have forgotten who they are and who and what we are here for.

"I am a Running bear of the Sioux tribe and would like to thank you for working with us and helping us to try and restore mother earth and the people and animals that are on this beautiful planet. Thank you for your assistance in this challenge and task that you have agreed to take part in. We will always be watching you, protecting you, and being by your side. We thank you for helping us.

But for now, rest as you have used much of your energy worrying about these things. We hope now you will be able to settle your mind and know we are always here for you.

Black Eagle, Running bear, and Navajo leaders and elders.

God bless."

Condor feathers

This message was a question I had a friend of mine ask me. She wanted me to ask my guides to answer a question for her. So, I said I would Ask my guides her question which was:

My condor feathers in the sun, when she is charging in the early sun, go into a rainbow state. Can you please advise?

She also has a shaman web page. She has no one in the group to speak about the rainbow children. She would like to offer you the opportunity to relay this information and any other information you would like to share onto her page, so to give you the opportunity to speak if you wish to and would like to know if you would like this opportunity. Please advise?

And that if you choose to accept this offer that it be channeled from a set chief.

Thank you.

Please advise.

The answer I received was:

Good evening to you all my chiefs and guides. I come to you with a question I have from a friend. She has a question for you and would like your guidance on this matter. Please come and assist me.

My friend asked me to ask you.

Her condors' feathers in the sun, when she is charging in the early sun go into a rainbow state, please can you advise her on this matter please.

"Good evening, Christine and welcome back to our table we would gladly help your friend.

The condor feathers that she speaks of will not charge in the sunlight as the condor is a bird of the night, she needs to charge them through the light of the moon. If she is to charge them through the light of the sun the heat will dry out the precious feathers and they will slowly start to deteriorate.

Regarding her offer regarding the rainbow children, we would gladly relay that information for her, we are here to help mother earth recover from the destruction that is being caused, we all need to stand together and join the fight to bring mother earth to her truly and rightful beauty. Her gifts have been slowly destroyed, she gave us all these gifts out of pure love, and they are all slowly being destroyed.

We all need to help people remember to learn to be in tune with the land, the elements, the sea, and all her beautiful creatures. We know you are nervous about what your friend has just asked you as it is a very new and scary opportunity, but we will happily guide you. You need to trust in what you hear and what you know, you are here to help the land and the animals recover we all here, we all need to go back to respecting mother earth she is upset and angered to what is happening to her land and beautiful animals, and we need to try and help her from this destruction that is being caused.

We can see you are beginning to doubt yourself. You do not need to be always supported by spirit in everything you do.

We are here to help you and guide you and we will help you learn to trust in what you receive. We understand that you are scared about what others might think and how they will respond to you, due to the bad comments you got before. We are here to help you, guide you and support you and help you through your journey, and we would very much like this opportunity to place our knowledge onto your friend's page. There is much information that needs to be related to many people and there are many people who will try to drag you down trust in your spiritual guidance and what you receive. We will help you, and help you gain that confidence once again you have had bad experiences in the past which are preventing you from moving forward and preventing you from believing in yourself.

The last question you asked we could not answer was you had to work that out for yourself, and we know this had a negative impact on your faith.

Your friend has presented you with an opportunity to rebuild that trust and we would very much like to take her up on her offer, but we cannot accept this offer without your valued support.

You asked a while ago what you were meant to do with the information, well this my friend is a good way to accept the help for that situation she can help you along with this on your path and we advise that you take up the opportunity as it would greatly help your own cause and ours. And we would very much like this opportunity but you also have free will and we would not stand in that's way so we will leave that decision for you to make. But it is a wonderful opportunity.

Just trust!!!!!"

General Reading

This piece of information was a card reading that I did for myself, and this is the response my guides gave me in reply to the reading.

"Good evening Christine, and welcome back to our table. We have seen you struggling and have come to assist you currently. You have seen many challenges of late, these are all challenges that need to be necessary for you to progress and Blume.

Your son is going through his own awakening currently, and we are very sorry that you have had to receive this recent trauma. He is currently learning a very important life lesson. He is learning the true meaning of love and respect. He will be learning how he needs to adjust his own actions in order to further his path. All will become clear soon. We know you have been struggling massively with this all you have many questions which we are unable to advise on but what we can tell you is that what is happening has been necessary, your friend Sasha is indeed right in what she says these are indeed not your own karmic lessons you are only part of the challenges.

Your son and son's dad must face. We are sorry for the trauma you are receiving currently, just continue to trust we are always working for your greatest and highest good, this is indeed the calm before the storm. You have indeed many challenges ahead but just please trust this is all part of the bigger part of the picture. You have many challenges ahead of you but also many rewards and much abundance coming to you, this is part of an initiation process that will lead you to your highest joy and happiness you have many blessings in your life at present and many more to come. I am here to help you and guide you along with all your other guides. We are here to help you along the way you will see the results of all your hard work and dedication not only to your son but to your purpose in general. We are Navajo elders, and we are your ancestral lineage you come from a line of wounded healers who were sent to this earth plan be to restore the love and balance within yourself and other people.

The shamanic path is not an easy route or path to follow but rest assured all the challenges you have faced have been for a reason. They have enabled you to help a lot of people due to your level of understanding within these situations and there are still many more people and animals that you will meet along your path we will help you and teach you and guide you to communicate the way you wish both through mediumship and animal communication so that you can fulfil your dreams of being able to help many more people along your path.

There is much work to be done and ahead for you all, but just stay true to your path, keep trusting and you will reap the rewards of what is to come.

Tanock is working with you, continuously helping you to restore your strength. Do not worry that you are not doing enough, you will receive the healing, help, and assistance that you need for you to succeed. You have many challenges ahead, but you are more than ready to deal with them. You are always divinely guided, and we will always be here for you, you are never alone, spirit will never give you more than you can manage just trust that all you are experiencing is to prepare you for what lies ahead, mother earth and the people, animals and crops are all in need of assistance and help.

The shaman's way will teach you to be as one with the land so that you may have access to the information and all materials things you will need to help you and assist you along the way. You are more than capable of dealing with what is ahead, but you must believe in yourself.

We can sit here and tell you how capable you are but unless you believe it yourself you will continue to struggle. We all lived through many challenges through our stay on the earth plane also and that enabled us to gain the knowledge we have in order to pass it on to you. Please believe in yourself.

We know Luke has played a massive part in you losing much of your energy and patience, confidence and self-esteem. He and your son have made you doubt yourself, who you are and what you are here to do, you do not need to. We are working with your son, Luke and Tarran and Taran will be with you soon, please do not feel you need to be worried in any way, he is getting stronger each day everything you spend time to heal you, you are also healing him. As you regain your personal power so does, he. He will be with you soon.

Sasha is also correct in what she thinks about the negatives, they will be needed, and they have been given as a gift for you also, as we know how important he is to you. We know you feel you have lost your time and feel that you will not be able to make up that time, or even try to make up that time, but trust us when we say you have nothing to fear. Taran has never forgotten the love you shared, not completely he has always had you in his heart like you, he forgot what true love really was, he too has faced many challenges within his life, he has also had to build himself up on many occasions. He has also been hurt many times but for different reasons which you will find out soon enough but for now just know that you are doing more than enough and as you get stronger, he is also getting stronger and seeing things clearer each day he will be with you soon, but just know he is ok. He will be here to show you himself soon just be patient, as everything must be in divine timing for everything to synch as it should but please just trust that you are doing enough and please stop doubting yourself. You know what is true within your heart, you always have. He is also looking forward to coming back but is also nervous and scared you have both been hurt and lead challenging lives. But he is ready to start a new chapter also and it will not be easy for either but just believe and trust you have been brought together for a reason, there is much work to be done, but you both needed to get strong again for the journey ahead and you have a new and exciting journey ahead. All will become clear soon just trust and believe in yourself and what you are here to do. There are many experiences to be learnt and understood ahead but believe that they are all here to help you learn, progress and grow. Keep trusting in what they are here to teach us, all the challenges and blessings are here to teach us to become who we are designed to become."

"I am Black eagle of the Cherokee tribe. I have been with you for a very long time. I am here to help teach you our medicines and our ways to help you learn and grow. Please help us to help you and bring you all you love and desire. We are all here to help guide you, we are pleased that you allowed your friend into your life. She is very wise and taught well shaman lines. She can teach you much to help you along your journey. She can teach you original ways and teachings she has learnt from her own elders and teachers. The question she asked you was indeed to test your answers as she has asked many people that question who have not turned out to be of true heart, we will test people to see if they can stay true to cause and purpose as the shaman way is by far not a challenge for someone who is not true to cause. There is powerful and medicinal knowledge which will be learned and can also be used in the wrong way. In the wrong hands it can be very powerful medicine and a shaman must face much pain and heartache as we need to take on that person's pains and fears in order to give them the healing that they need. These are our own precious teachings and need to be sure that you are true to heart and spirit and the cause and purpose. You are here to do. But you have past all your challenges and tasks set for you and have stayed true to heart and cause and we would very much like to continue with your path and continue to guide and teach you our knowledge and ways as you have proved time and time again that you wish to continue those teaching for the right reasons. You have shown time and time again to show you can stay true to your cause and purpose on this earth plane and hope that you will continue to allow us into your life so we may continue to teach you. Work with your friend, learn how to gain the knowledge that you seek, we will continue to teach you and teach you our ways and we will look forward to working with you on your journey.

Thank you for allowing us this opportunity to continue to assist you along your path.

Thank you and God bless."

Black Eagle

Animal Communication

Good evening my chiefs and elders, what is it you wish to share with us this evening.

"I am running bear, good evening. I have come to give you some of the answers to some of your questions that you have recently been asking. I am here to help you and guide you in request.

You have been asking many questions recently, I am glad you enjoyed your conversation with the horses the other day. The reason they responded to you is because you said that you wished to help them, all those horses believe in you and what you are here to do, but you do not have a lot of faith in yourself.

So I have come to reassure you, you really do not have anything to fear, you picked up everything violet was telling you today she was indeed frightened you have connected with her on a spiritual level although you didn't not necessarily realize you did, you are correct in what you are sensing and feeling and she does indeed wish to work with you, but she also understands Lucy has in fact put a stop to that she was deeply disappointed to that affect but also you are in a difficult position and there is not a lot of things you have and can do about that this she wants you to know she is very grateful for your love and respect, for her and is she is

43

grateful that you can see the things she says and doe, and that you listen, you listen and she understands that you have tried and is very happy that you came into her life and helped her feel love. You have indeed restored her faith in humans and want to thank you for caring and are upset that you have to leave but also understand you have to help yourself get better. She wants to thank you for helping her feel safe today when Charles upset her. She doesn't understand why Charles doesn't like her and why he doesn't want her to be a part of the herd but also understands you cared for and loved her, and she is very grateful for that. She just wanted to let her tell you that before you left and to let you know that she will miss you but wanted to let you know that she loves you too. She knows the others do not understand her like you do and she wants you to know that and wanted to say that she is grateful for you listening and trying to get the others to understand. She knows you know how she was feeling in the stable today and wanted to say thank you for noticing but not to give up on what you do, she wants you to continue the good work that you do, and to tell you to stop doubting yourself as you don't need to. You are a very special person and she knows you are here to help her and all the others but she just wanted you to know you are very well thought of by her and she thanks you for the love you have shown she will be eternally grateful and she also said she also knows she reminds you of Annie and wanted to tell you Annie is fine and she will always be fine because her time with you also restored her faith in humans as you have done for her, and wants you to know she loves you very much and not to worry about her and that she will be fine as you are only next door but to say thank you for loving her the way you did."

Inner Child Healing message

27-07-18

Good evening to my chiefs and guides, I would like to call upon your assistance if I may.

My question for you tonight is?

How can I heal the child I lost in my previous lifetime? What can you tell me about the child, and is the healing of this child linked to the challenges I have with my children in this lifetime?

Please come and assist me now and help me to find the answers to these questions if you may. I thank you for your assistance in this matter as I would like to continue my healing process so that I may be able to assist other people within these matters who have had similar experiences. I wish to continue with my healing process and would like your assistance with this. So please come and help me now.

"Well good evening Christine and thank you for allowing us to assist you in this matter we can indeed tell you are right in your thinking that you have indeed lost a child in a previous lifetime with your twin flame Taran we can tell you that you lost this child within the 1700's, the child had been sick for a while due to the poverty and resistance that was going on at the time. At the time you were indeed a Navajo, this was the tribe you were part of at the time, you and Taran have been together through many lifetimes you have been through many traumas throughout your lifetimes. The child was a little girl she was indeed very pretty, a real little princess you were both very proud of her, but unfortunately the lack of food that was around at the time indeed made her very sick, a lot of people were lost at that time and a lot of heartache and trauma have been caused at this time you were deeply upset by this trauma and you have indeed carried the pain of this trauma through many lifetimes. The reason you are asking this question at this time is because there are indeed other things linked to this situation. You have suffered many years of feeling the loss of your little bundle of joy and part of the reason you have been drawn to Sams charity and her cause is so that you can try to help the other youngsters because you had no way of helping the little girl that you lost and have carried the guilt of that for many years and this is partly why you feel so guilty about what has happened to your children in this lifetime, it has been very difficult for you to accept what has happened and you struggled to understand as you do now as to how to help or rectify that situation and I can see you have concerns that may not be able to help that child but what you need to know and what you need to realize is, as you heal your own inner child, you are also healing that child, Taran and yourself. The more healing work you do on yourself will automatically filter through to the other two, Taran and that child. I know this has been a difficult piece of information for you to accept, as losing a child is always incredibly traumatic. This is why when you had your ectopic child you struggled so badly with the loss as it brought back the hidden trauma of the loss of the other child also but subconsciously not consciously but you were not aware of this ect the time and children that we lose over our lifetimes is a difficult cross to bear, the reason the child was lost or any child is lost is because that child also has its own lessons and quest that it has to achieve the arrangement for when that child is to leave this earth plane is already pre anticipated and agreed before that child gets incarnated, what we find hard to understand is the "why?" and we carry the guilt of this as it is all part of being human and feeling those emotions, what you need to focus on is the fact that the healing you do on yourself, will always filter through to that child. You do not need to continue to feel the guilt of losing any of the children you did have, or lost, as we said earlier, they already decided on their cause and purpose and that child has its own path to walk and when that child left their incarnation it was already. pre anticipated, so you do not need to carry that guilt anymore, as the main purpose of it has now been identified, you wished to find the child and heal it, but you do not need to as she lives within you always and you have been triggered now to do the needed work within your own inner child as you know it will help that child to also heal. So yes to a certain extent the child has had an impact on the challenges you have with your own current children as the guilt had been carried down for many lifetimes but as the child you lost your current children also have their own purpose and pre-arranged plans and purpose which they have also pre-arranged so the lesson here as you have already found the answer to you know and understand that your children have their own lessons and purpose. They have chosen to learn. They have their own agenda and lessons they must learn and have chosen to learn so again do not carry the guilt of thinking you are to blame in any way of your current situation as your children have already their path and you are all agreed before you came here to help each other reach the lessons they each individually wanted to learn. Your children have already chosen their paths they are walking and it's their choice as to what path they chose to take, you can try to guide them as we guide you, but they will decide which way they choose to go and choose how they want to learn those lessons. Your youngest also chose his own path before he came, and you had all agreed to be part of that soul group to help each other learn the lessons each other wishes to learn and this is the way that you chose to help each other. We may not necessarily understand, who chooses to choose the way that they have chosen all you need to understand is that you are here to walk your own path you all have the lessons you have chosen to learn, so you do not need to feel guilty about any of it. All that you can do is try your best to walk the path that you have chosen to walk and that is what you need to focus on at this time.

We are here to help guide you and assist you and we will always be happy to assist you in these matters and all other matters you wish us to help you with. We thank you for allowing us to help you and hope that this has helped answer the questions that you asked of us."

"I am crow man of the Sioux tribe and I thank you for helping us in our quest and allowing us to help and assist you on your quest, we look forward to speaking with you again soon. Thank you for giving us this opportunity God bless you and goodnight."

Cleansing ritual to help heal the land

01-09-18

Good evening Spirit and my Chiefs, Angels, Ancestors, and supporting network. I call upon you now and ask that you share your knowledge and wisdom with me this evening to help and assist me in the following question.

Can you please tell me if there is anything specific that I can do to clear my house and heal the land?

Please come and assist me with this question.

What is it that I can do, to help with the situation?

I wish to know this due to me wishing to progress on my journey and help me to get better as I feel the house may be on ground that is not particularly happy.

What is it that I can specifically do to help the land to heal from the trauma and destruction it has suffered?

I wish to clear my house of all negative energy held within the land area and county it has been built on from this lifetime, and all other lifetimes from the day it was created by the beautiful mother earth. How and what do I need to do in order to achieve this. Please give me your love and guidance so I can try to heal the land from its suffering. Please come and assist me now in this matter.

"Good evening Christine and welcome back to our table.

I am Running bear of the Sioux tribe and we are very grateful to be able to help and assist you in this matter. You are indeed correct in what you feel and think and this land has indeed suffered much suffering we as a tribe are very passionate about healing our precious mother earth and the heartache she has suffered and would be very grateful if you could help and assist us in our quest to try and heal the land the way in which is to do, this is to bless and consecrate the ground. We would be happy to assist you in the ritual and process sin order to do this.

You will require several blessings for mother earth these are required for all of the elements of the land. Earth, Water, Fire and Air.

In order for the ritual to work we need to be able to submit the blessings into the land, choose a spot which is sacred to you. Be it a place you like to sit and meditate or a place you feel appropriate at the time. In order to consecrate the ground, ask the Great Spirit for protection for you and all of mankind throughout the process and call upon his power to be able to consecrate and bless the ground in which you live, the surrounding area, and throughout the entire land in which you live. Ask for all the plants, animals, living beings, humans and animals to be blessed and given the power of the Great Spirit to Cleanse, Clear, and transmute all negative energy within their being and their auric field and ask that all negative energy be cleansed, cleared and transmuted into positive loving energy, and ask that, that energy that is positive and pure be placed back into the beautiful mother earth and all of her creations and ask that she be supported, loved, treasured, and appreciated for all that she has given us as we are all part of the same circle of life. We are all part of the Great Spirit, all created of the same blood, and lifeforce, and ask that the Great Spirit radiate out its loving spirit to every person, creature, plant and animal within, on, above, below surrounding and living upon the mother earth and ask that she may be renewed, regenerated, and cleansed, cleared, blessed, and give thanks to her and all she has created and proceed in order for us all to be able to grow, evolve, and enjoy our life experience, upon her soul.

Thank the Great Spirit for his assistance in this matter and place the gifts you have brought for her upon the land and ask that she may take the gifts as a token of your love, grace, and beauty and thank her for producing and giving the love that she has for us all upon this planet. Water, A candle, A feather and some tobacco as your gifts for her.

Leave the gifts for her overnight, and you shall see she will, accept, the gifts and bring great blessings, into her life and into yours. She will clear all the negativity within your land and will greatly appreciate your blessings and love which you have conveyed onto her and will be very happy.

Always be sure to ask for the Great Spirits protection and he will always love, guide and protect you always from now and until you leave this lifetime, he will continue to love you, guide you, and protect you as we will.

If you do this great blessing mother earth will greatly appreciate it. There is much work to be done and with your help and assistance we will be able to become one step closer to the achieving our goal as you will be one step closer to your goals."

"Also, you asked earlier in your head, what is it that you were specifically here for.

Your purpose is to help and assist us and the earth to help and recover from the destruction caused.

You are here to help with that by helping, healing, and assisting the animals of the planet to be given a voice. You are here to help Mother Earths beautiful animals feel valued once again, to feel loved, respected and listened to once again. You will find a way to help the rainbow children of this planet reach a new understanding and be shown a different way, you will show the children and the animals they are and will be respected by showing the new generations the true meaning of life and help them to see and realize that just because you have been treated a particular way doesn't mean that you have to continue that cycle of destruction. The healing you have done on yourself has already and will continue to do, will show people and children alike that everyone is in control of their own destiny as their own life lessons they wish to learn and that how they choose to do that is their own choice, but you will show them there is a better way, through love, prayer, consistency, determination, and love. You will show them there is a better way and we are all part of the one cycle of life. People have forgotten what loyalty, honesty, appreciation, gratitude, and love can achieve when you all stand together as one together instead of being isolated.

Isolation is good for receiving guidance and sometimes is indeed needed, but people have forgotten what it is to be part of a community, to work together for a bigger cause and work as one instead of being divided through money, power, and competitiveness. You are one of not very many who have not forgotten the true values, principals, and honor. Many people who now live on this planet have forgotten that we need to remind people of the hidden and forgotten knowledge that our ancestors have for us. They are here to remind us, help us, guide us, and try to restore the people and the land to how it should be, to remind people of who they are and the great resource they came from. People need to be reminded that the land and animals need to be respected, they have been given to us out of gifts of pure love from mother earth and she is greatly upset by what and how her beautiful land and people have become. We need people like yourself to help us along our path as well as helping you along your path as we are no longer in the physical plane but have much knowledge, love, respect, and understanding for all our brothers and sisters alike that are upon the land we are here to guide you and show you our teachings and ways to help and assist you along your way, and will be always here to guide you and help you upon your journey. We are truly grateful and blessed that you have chose to help us upon our cause as well as accepting the path of your cause also.

We will teach you and guide you in how to best achieve your goals, if we can, and will always be here to help and guide you with any questions you may have for us.

"I am the Crow man of the Sioux tribe and would like to thank you for helping us in this matter and I would like to thank you for Agreeing to help us with our quest. We are very sad about what we are seeing happen to our beautiful mother earth it causes us much distress having to watch her cry her tears to what has happened to her beautiful planet she is very sad but also angry and also grateful for your service to this cause we look forward to watching you grow and evolve into the beautiful light that you are.

Animal Communication

"We know you are worried about violet. She is indeed in great distress , she is unfortunately not very happy at this time but she knows you love her very much , she knows you can hear her and she knows you want her to be with you, she knows its distressing you very much knowing she is not happy but as long as you continue to love her she knows she is loved, cared for, respected, and listened to and as long as she knows all of the above she will be able to cope I know this upsets you clearly as you love her very much. She will in time be ok. Charles is indeed a very troubled soul; he is just not very good at trying to lead a herd. He will settle down eventually. I know you care about all of those horses and it is indeed a shame that they haven't got an owner as understanding and loving as you, but rest assured all of those horses even Charles knows that you love them and Charles knows that when you say you hate him he knows you don't mean it as he also knows how much love you have for all of those horses and how much you tried to show their owners the right way but unfortunately they will all have their own lessons they have chosen to learn and unfortunately they are a long way from wanting to listen but rest assured the horses have their own ideas of what's going to happen and sooner or later their owners will learn that there way is not necessarily the right way, and in the meantime the horses are very capable of making sure them being hurt will be tolerated and they will help their owners see the right way forward. All horses are here to help restore the balance, as are you and balance, love, and respect will be restored eventually if people like yourself keep wanting to try and make this world a better place.

All those horses know what you are here to do and what you are here for, and they are all waiting to help you and guide you also. Make yourself better , concentrate on that for now and then you will be able to help those horses, as you will be better able to hear what they have to say and yes it was indeed Annie who come to see you the other night, you were correct in the fact you felt it was her energy she was and is very fond of you and she wanted to come check you were ok. She knew and realized you were in distress and sensed you were upset and she wanted to come and help you feel at ease and show you that you were loved and supported too as she is very grateful for the love that you gave to her, when she was with you and wanted to let you know she was ok as she knows you were distressed about violet and knows violet reminds you of her, but unfortunately you are not in a position to help violet like you did her, as she is Lucys. But just know that violet knows she is loved, and she knows you are there for her and she knows you will always love her as she will you, and just by being there, noticing, how she is feeling and paying attention means more to her than any attention her owners can give her. She has a spiritual connection with you as do the other horses, and she knows she is loved and that gives her all the strength she needs to know you and h love her the way you do means everything. All the horses you come across will all realize you are here to help them and all of them appreciate it.

You have many more animals and horses you will come across in this lifetime and each one of them will be given a voice as they will know that you can heal them and help them. All the horses you come across will all see what a beautiful person you are and will see your intentions loud and clear and they will all feel loved and find their inner strength they need in order to face whatever challenges their humans present them with, because they know they will have your love and support to help them cope and they will also help you to cope with life and deal with the challenges you will be presented with as they are also healers as you know from wild horse. He still has many lessons to teach you and teach you and he will help you heal and get better. He will be there to support you all the way as you supported him.

I hope this has helped answer some of your questions that you seek."

"I am running bear of the Sioux tribe and we wish you a very blessed and loving night's sleep now, as you are tired and you need your rest, take your time to get better as you still have many blessings and challenges, and battles ahead, but you will succeed in all of them as we are here to help you and guide you. With the greatest love and respect, we wish you a good night, God bless, and we will speak with you again soon.

God bless"

Communications from the horses I have come across in my lifetime so far

Bryan

I believe all animals are spiritual beings with their own souls, and their own learning paths. I believe animals should have mutual respect and are all wise teachers who can teach us many things if we choose to listen, they can teach us much medicine if we open our hearts and choose to listen to the knowledge and wisdom, they have to teach us.

I would like to now call in my guides Running bear and Francis of Assisi and ask for their assistance in helping me to communicate with the horses at my yard, as I feel they have things they wish to say before I leave, and I would like very much to give them the voice they deserve for them to feel heard and get their messages across.

I would like to start, if possible, with Bryan as I feel he has the most to say and has many things burdening his mind so I would like to call Bryan now and ask him if he would like to communicate with me. He can say as little or as much as he wants to say, and if wishes to communicate I would greatly like to hear what he has to say.

"Good evening Christine and welcome back to our table. Thank you for returning to us and allowing us to help you.

I am Running bear of the Sioux tribe and would gladly help you in helping you to communicate with the animals. You are indeed correct, Bryan would indeed like to speak with you. He would like to thank you for showing the kindness that you have towards him, he is indeed worried About his friend Jackson he is one of his comrades he has worked with in his past and he feels there is something wrong and wishes Kelly to try and trace his owner and find out how he is doing he feels that he may be poorly and wants Kelly to check on him He is showing Bryan his tummy area, and feels there may be a problem. He would also like Kelly to know that he loves her very much and he misses her, he enjoys his hacks out and he wants her to know that he is very happy she is his owner but that he is not very ready to retire just yet, he would like to give some more as she brings him much love and enjoys spending time with her. He wants me to tell her he would like to give her a pink rose, to show how much he loves her, as he knows that she likes pink roses not red and that he has enjoyed the many years of service with her, that he is very proud of her and that he loves her very much and that he is not a big fan of the garlic. He prefers carrots. He would really like her to try and find out how Jackson is as he misses him very much and the others from the force and would really like a catch up to be organized so he could see them all again as he was very proud to walk by their sides. He would like to leave his love there and would like to thank you for taking the time to hear his message. He is very grateful."

I would like to thank Bryan for his message and to let him know I will pass the message on.

Bruno

The next horse I would like to speak to which I feel has something to say is Bruno, as I feel he has something to say also.

"Good morning Christine, and thank you for coming back to our table. Thank you for assisting us in this cause.

Can you please tell me what Bruno has to say.

"Your pendulum is indeed right, and Bruno would indeed like to speak to you. I am Running bear of the Sioux tribe and am honored to be able to help and assist you in this task. Bruno is very pleased that you have came here and will be very sad to see you go but he understands why you have to go as he understands henry needs to be a part of a herd he would like to tell you that he is very grateful for the help love and assistance you have gave him and he wants you to tell Donna that he loves her very much and the children and he is looking very forward to her plan in the springtime he is very much looking forward to being part of the family and being ridden again he said he will miss his rides out with sandy as he has always preferred company when he is being ridden and he is sorry he is such a scaredy cat. He said when he was a young foal before Donna had him and he was left for very long periods of time on his own and he had no older horses to help him to feel secure or loved he developed his fears very young and has tried and will try very hard to get over his fears he is very sorry for all the times he almost made donna falloff due to this and he is sorry he scared her when she first had him it's because he had to look after himself from a very young age and it made him aggressive as a form of defense mechanism. He is very sorry that he scared her and to let her know the reason he pins people in the stable is also due to the treatment he suffered before Donna got him. He wants you to tell Donna he apologizes for all the fear he caused her and very much wants to make it up to herby showing her he can be a safe boy and he knows that donna will take the time and care to help him overcome his fear she wants to say he loves her very much and wants to give her a bunch of red roses with a red ribbon and a red heart on the ribbon to show her how much, he loves her very much and understands she cannot be around as much now and he is looking forward to working with her again he would also like to thank Vicky for helping him to overcome his fears also and he is sorry she has been so poorly and would like to tell donna to send his love to Vicky and to say thank you for helping him in his time of need and he hopes she gets better soon. He would also like to ask if he can have some swede in his dinner as it is his favorite vegetable. He would like to thank Donna for her devoted love to him over the years and he hopes to be working with her again soon. That is all he wishes to say for now x"

Hunny

"I have Hunny here and she would like to give a message to Katie and Julia. She would like to thank them both for being so kind to her and to thank the rescue center who helped her and rescued her from those terrible conditions, she said it was horrible having to watch her friends suffer. She especially misses her friend called Bella. They had been together since they were born but unfortunately, she was too weak She wants to say how grateful she is to Julia for taking her in and she knows it was a difficult decisions Julia wasn't planning on having any more ponies, but she is very grateful. She wants to say that even though she does miss Boris, she would like to say a very big thank you to Katie for bringing Tally over to her. She misses Jimmy very much as he helped her very much, he helped her feel safe and secure and she misses him very much although he used to bully her a little when she first came and all his antics, but she misses him very much. She said when Jimmy died it brought back all the trauma, she had witnessed from losing her other friends and that's why she went mad whinnying and being restless in the paddock because she got scared again. She would like to thank Julia and Katie for their kindness and she is very happy she now lives with them and she hopes Julia will continue to come down and see her once the donkeys come and that would very much like to meet them when they do come she said she really enjoyed her walk out with Tally and Katie, and would very much like to go out for more walks now her feet all be it still a little sore they are a lot better now and would like to go out again as she likes being able to see the world and would maybe like a little rider one day but will see, but for now she wants send you both her love and would like to give you a box of roses to share as she knows you are both not big fans of flowers She would also like to send her love to Jim and wants to tell him to continue to be brave and she is proud of Jim and Julia for overcoming the trauma they have also suffered she understands your worries and she hopes he will feel better soon and was happy to see Jim up and about. She wants to leave her love there and would like to say thank you and she loves you very much x"

"I am Running Bear of the Sioux tribe and would like to thank you personally from myself and our tribes to thank you for your kindness love and honour, your loyalty to yours and our causes has been highly noted and you will soon see and reap the rewards and fruits of your labour soon. Please do not worry the Great Spirit has been very pleased with your dedication to your cause. We are honored to be able to thank you for allowing us to help you alonmg your path and look very forward to working with you again soon. Now get some rest as your energy needs renewing we will indeed send you some healing when you sleep along with some courage, strenghth, and determination so when you wake you willfeel renewed and ready to fight another day. Thank you again for allowing us to help, support, and guide you. God bless you x."

Printed in the USA
CPSIA information can be obtained
at www.ICGtesting.com
LVHW022208200124
769329LV00004B/490